ROPHECIES, PRAYERS & DECLARATIONS

# PROVISION

## SHAWN BOLZ

Published by ICreate Productions,
PO Box 50219, Studio City, CA 91614
www.bolzministries.com

To contact the author about speaking at your conference or church,
please go to www.bolzministries.com

Edited by Kyle Duncan

ISBN: 978-1-952421-01-3

eBook ISBN: 978-1-952421-02-0

Printed in the United States of America

# TABLE OF CONTENTS

*"So Abraham called the name of that place, 'Jehovah-Jireh, The Lord will provide'; as it is said to this day, 'On the mount of the Lord **it shall be provided.**'"*

**Genesis 22:14**

*If you listen obediently to the Voice of God, your*
*God, and heartily obey all his commandments*
*that I command you today, God, your God, will*
*place you on high, high above all the nations of*
*the world. All these blessings will come down on*
*you and spread out beyond you because you have*
*responded to the Voice of God, your God:*

*God's blessing inside the city,*
*God's blessing in the country;*
*God's blessing on your children,*
*the crops of your land,*
*the young of your livestock,*
*the calves of your herds,*
*the lambs of your flocks.*
*God's blessing on your basket and bread bowl;*
*God's blessing in your coming in,*
*God's blessing in your going out.*

Psalm 40:3 (TPT)

# HOW TO USE
# THIS BOOK

## WHY POWER OF PROPHECIES, PRAYERS, AND DECLARATIONS?

Throughout human history we have seen prayer, the prophetic, and declarations shape societies, set culture, provide heritage, and bring vision for the future. I wrote this book so that you would have a very specific tool to help you use words to define your own history and future with God. I love the power of prayer, prophecy, and declaration. These have been weapons in my own life that created the context of faith and intimacy I am now living in. I see these three expressions as some of the most important tools for defining our relationships, vision, and calling in life.

Prophecy is God's will—accompanied by His love—declared over us. It gives us an opportunity to align our faith in conviction with what we believe about ourselves. It helps our mind, will, and emotions catch up to His Spirit. Prophecy creates vision for the gap between what is not yet happening and what God desires to do in our lives, and it helps us engage a process of relationship with God, through faith, to close that gap. It changes our opportunities, ignites our potential, and causes us to have a chance to live beyond the fruit we can attain by our own efforts.

Prayer helps us commune with God's nature and heart. We get to converse with God with listening ears. We get to share our pain, victory, struggles, and inner life with God. Through prayer, we allow the Holy Spirit to share God's heart and we experience being one with Him.

Declarations are when we speak out loud, on purpose, for a purpose. These are our statements of faith aligning us to God's will and directives for our lives and the world around us.

Life is in the power of the tongue. "Death and life are in the power of the tongue, and those who love it will eat its fruit" (Proverbs 18:21 NKJV). As Christians, and as emotionally intelligent humans, we see that the tongue is our most powerful tool or weapon. It has power to release life wherever we go. People who understand this will speak intentionally and will eat the abundant fruit their past words (declarations) have produced. We will speak words of life to others and to ourselves, because we realize that silence is indifference and passivity is a thief. Declarations help us be intentional and, therefore, aware of when God does move, because we are declaring and then looking for the fulfillment of our declarations.

When you combine prayers, declarations, and prophecies—like you will encounter in this book—you become even more intentional about the power of words. In the book of Joel, the author shares a prophetic picture of a group of people experiencing a revelation of the time and season in which they were living. It says that they beat their plowshares into swords and their pruning hooks into spears. That is what I hope to accomplish here, in this book. Let the words that you have used to cultivate faith in your identity, calling, and destiny now become weapons as you speak them out over yourself and everyone around you.

Words are weapons that propel us forward to lay hold of all that Jesus won for us. "Your very words will be used as evidence against you, and your words will declare you either innocent or guilty" (Matthew 12:37 TPT). This verse is not talking about being saved through godly words, but it does imply that our declarations will either restrict or bless our lives. Instead of setting up boundaries of limitation and restriction in our lives (allowing words to condemn us or declare us guilty), using our words deliberately will propel us into the abundant life Jesus promised us.

Prophecies, prayers, and declarations are instrumental for us to enter our promised land.

"Always remember what is written in that book of law. Speak about that book and study it day and night. Then you can be sure to obey what is written there. If you do this, you will be wise and successful in everything you do" (Joshua 1:8 ERV).

God spoke to Joshua and told him to continually speak the truth as he made final preparations to grab hold of what God had already promised him. Joshua is our example, teaching us how to use prayers, declarations, and prophetic words as a means to possessing the promises of God.

Using prayer, prophecies, and declarations to activate our faith for things that don't yet exist in our lives is one of the greatest ways we can be like our model, Jesus.

"For in God's presence he believed that God can raise the dead and call into being things that don't even exist yet" (Romans 4:17 TPT).

As a Christian, you aren't only aware of injustice or brokenness, you are aware of the fact that through Jesus, anything can be redeemed or restored. You start to understand the Spirit of God is focused on bringing life to dead places, people, nations, gifts, and calls.

You also get to see into His heart and original plan or intention in everything He created. Through this, you will begin to have the opportunity to speak to situations, people, and purposes calling forth what doesn't even exist yet.

We see a lot of scriptural examples of people using prophetic words, prayers, and declarations as a verbal tool in their relationship with their faith and connection to God, themselves, and the world.

Through this book, I am inviting you on a journey of learning how to use words to speak into the very fabric of your life, the spiritual realm, and the world around you. These words are tools to help you align your faith and create an inner life full of courage and hope. You will find yourself using your own language at times or tailoring the words I have written for yourself, and that is exactly what you should do! Make it apply deeply and closely to you and your situation!

Words create space and need space to be created, so I would encourage you to utilize this book in times when you are alone or with a partner, and allow the words to be spoken out loud. If you don't feel faith when you are saying a declaration, say it again and again, and allow the words to become more familiar to your heart. If you can't own the goodness of one of the prophetic words, repeat it with your name in it so that it's yours. With prayers, make sure you aren't just religiously repeating what is on paper but actually picture yourself in the prayer. These are your tools, your words, and you must own them and make them work for you. Eventually, as you read this, you will even beat these words into weapons, and you will see results.

Practically, the book is laid out over several areas of life, and we are using the theme of God's provision to empower your faith in each area. No one section is quite the same because I didn't want to give you a formula, but rather, help you develop language and some models for how to use the powerful tools of prophecy, prayers, and declarations. The way we declare in one area of life might seem totally different to the next. Sometimes the prophecies are written in first person, sometimes they are written as the stated intention of God as I have received it for you.

How you choose to read this book is up to you. Maybe you need the specific subject heading to guide you, or maybe you want to visit each section in order as you prophesy, declare, and pray into your life. Maybe some sections won't feel authentic to the way you express yourself or it just won't apply directly to your life right now. If that is the case, don't get hung up but keep moving forward and find the words that will help you gain greater breakthrough in your life.

I pray that you will find yourself using and reusing this book as you hear God speak to your heart. I would encourage you to underline specific phrases in each section that you are coming into agreement with. Say the prayers until they are your prayers. Own the prophecies, because they are for you. Make declarations with your family and say them until they are part of your DNA. Most of all, let this be your book as if you wrote each word yourself.

# INTRODUCTION TO PROVISION

God is a Father, and a Father's nature is to provide for His family. Everything we need, before we even think of it, God has a provision. As a matter of fact, for every destiny God created us with, there is a plan of full provision accompanying it. When God gives us a purpose or relationship or connection to someone, He has built in the ability to create the resources so that it can come into His full plan. In other words, provision is never the vision or the goal of God, it is His resource to walk out His heart and bring about everything you would need to reach and develop yourself, the family, and people that God has called you to.

This nature of God revealing who He is as a provider is in one of the most foundational biblical stories: Abraham and Isaac. God had asked Abraham to sacrifice his one and only son but right before the moment of Abraham's obedience, an angel came.

"But the angel of the Lord called to him from heaven and said, 'Abraham, Abraham!' And he said, 'Here I am.' He said, 'Do not lay your hand on the boy or do anything to him, for now I know that you fear God, seeing you have not withheld your son, your only son, from me.' And Abraham lifted up his eyes and looked, and behold, behind him was a ram, caught in a thicket by his horns. And Abraham went and took the ram and offered it up as a burnt offering instead of his son. So Abraham called the name of that place, '(Jehovah-Jireh) The Lord will provide'; as it is said to this day, 'On the mount of the Lord it shall be provided'" (Genesis 22:11–14).

God the provider, Jehovah Jireh, gave life. He saved the promised son from being a sacrifice. He preserved His promise to make Isaac a great nation. He acted faithfully in response to Abraham's faith in His provision. He was also showing a picture that He wasn't asking us to make the ultimate sacrifice but He was going to do it for us in giving the life of His own son, Jesus so that we could have full reconnection to Him as a Father.

We see God demonstrate this with the Israelites in multiple ways all through the Old Testament. Two most notable ways I want to focus on come from Deuteronomy 8:18 when God speaks that the ability to produce resource and wealth comes from Him, and it is directly linked to His nature over His chosen people. Then again with Bezalel in Exodus 31 where God anointed Bezalel to be able to have the creativity, artistic ability, and skill to create with all the resources that God was bringing Israel to worship Him.

For every vision there is a provision. Resources, prosperity, money, are not the destiny of God's people, although they are part of our benefit. When we start to see what God had in store for those who love Him, it is not wealth or resources, it is walking in full connection to Him and our self and the world around us. He provides so we can live fully, much as a parent provides so that their children can fully develop.

Obviously Christianity has seen its fair share of imbalance in the area of provision and finances. The hyper wealth movement where everyone gets to be rich has caused so much damage. At the same time, the socialistic or even poverty mindset are the other end of the pendulum of imbalance. To the spiritually intelligent it is easy to see that heresy is often truth out of balance. A person can take a legitimate biblical truth and emphasize it so much that he ignores other biblical truths that balance it. This doctrine that has been pushed out of balance is the truth that God provides abundantly for His people. It is a precious truth, taught throughout the Bible. So many people have taken that teaching and combined it with greed and materialism so that they teach that extreme wealth is the God-given right of every believer and this has also caused severe confusion.

There have been countless people who have preyed on the desire to come out of poverty and brokenness through immediate miracles and this creates the overindulgent false wealth and hyper prosperity movement. So many wealthy people even in Christianity are not blessed but have a lot of material goods. Having stuff is not blessing. Cooperating with God in a way that causes prosperity of soul and Spirit creates a blessed life in the natural. At the same time one third of Christianity lives in poverty and a lot of these impoverished people are not able to dream about what it would be like to be fully provided for and resourced past survival.

We need to look at the message of God richly providing for His people in the Bible. Whether it comes in the form as an extreme to the more balanced resource and wealth messages out there you can weigh it against this:

**Do you need this resource to bring Jesus His reward and fulfill your destiny of loving the people He is calling you to?**

This will balance out each time as you are learning to steward His abundance and resource.

For the sake of some of you reading this, we need to make sure that our overreaction to some of the hyper wealth message doesn't make the pendulum swing to the other extreme. Whenever there is a false teaching, there is the danger that we will overreact by neglecting the true doctrine. When false teachers say that extreme prosperity is the divine right of every Christian, there is the danger that we will neglect the comforting truth that God does provide, not just the minimum, but as Paul expresses it, "exceeding abundantly beyond all that we ask or think" (Eph. 3:20). Or in the Passion Translation: "God can do anything, you know—far more than you could ever imagine or guess or request in your wildest dreams! He does it not by pushing us around but by working within us, his Spirit deeply and gently within us."

I love how the Bible is full of examples of God's abundant provision for His people. Whether it was for taxes: Matthew 17:27: "But so that we may not cause offense, go to the lake and throw out your line. Take the first fish you catch; open its mouth and you will find a four-drachma coin. Take it and give it to them for my tax and yours." Or the donkey the Father provided for Jesus to ride in to fulfill prophetic Scripture in Matthew 21:2–3: saying to them, "Go to the village ahead of you, and at once you will find a donkey tied there, with her colt by her. Untie them and bring them to me. If anyone says anything to you, say that the Lord needs them, and he will send them right away."

We see these miraculous examples of how everything that is needed is there.

When you begin to see God as a provider and that it comes from His Father's heart then you also become a provider on the Earth. You come not just to receive but to give.

I remember when we first moved to Los Angeles, it was in the middle of the recession of 2007 and there was also an entertainment strike that was long-lasting and put the entertainment industry in peril. Most of our people worked in the entertainment industry or were transplants to LA. I remember one night we were expressing so much need that it seemed to endless. God spoke to my heart as I cried out to Him for our church, city, and nation. "You don't need me to come and just rescue you, you need me to help change the culture of your mind and heart. You don't need a provider right now, I have given you the ability to produce resources in the hardest places on Earth. Everyone comes to LA to get something, a career, fame, education, but I have commissioned you to give something. You are called to be benefactors and release finances and resources."

We were struggling to pay rent on our building, I was struggling to make it month to month even in my personal bills. But this changed everything. We literally repented of wanting a sugar daddy to come rescue us or some human being to just bail us out. We began to take on our rightful Kingdom mindset that just as the Father is a provider and benefactor and waymaker, that is who we are supposed to be as well. We are supposed to do what we see the Father doing.

A friend of mine in that season had me read all the parables and said, "What if you represent the Father in these stories? Like the parable of the lost son who squanders everything and the jealous brother. What if you aren't supposed to see yourself as one or the other, but as the Father who gives back the inheritance to the prodigal and who nurtures the jealous brother's heart helping him to understand?" This changed everything for us! Because as a church, as a leadership team, and me individually I began to see myself as someone who could be a resourcer, not just someone who needed resource. That is who God is and that is who He wants to make you.

It started little at first. One month, I gave a mother groceries. Then I paid for her daycare for a month and gave her more groceries. That wasn't rare for me in life but in the recession season it felt almost stupid to take what little I had and share it with someone. That second month a film crew came and asked if they could use our rental house for a project for an independent film. The owner said, "Have them rent it and you keep the money. I want you blessed." They paid us enough for the rest of our time in that house. Each time I took on the nature of Jehovah Jireh, I began to see both sides of provision, the need fulfilled and also becoming like Him to fulfill others.

## GOD BRINGS PROVISION IN ABUNDANCE FOR OUR NEEDS FROM HIS FATHER'S NATURE

God brings provision in abundance for all our needs. As I said before, God's primary nature is first a Father. Jesus even compares Him to natural fathers on Earth saying in Matthew 6:(TPT) "'This is why I tell you to never be worried about your life, for all that you need will be provided, such as food, water, clothing—everything your body needs. Isn't there more to your life than a meal? Isn't your body more than clothing? Look at all the birds—do you think they worry about their existence? They don't plant or reap or store up food, yet your heavenly Father provides them each with food. Aren't you much more valuable to your father than they?"

God created our life and knows we need resources to live it and we need to know Him as the one who provides. Jehovah Jireh is not just a buzzword or a nice name, it is part of His nature that you can access. He will abundantly provide for all our needs—material, emotional, and spiritual.

## PROSPERITY IS NOT OUR DIVINE RIGHT BUT WE DO GET BLESSED

I love the story that Pastor Bill Johnson tells about how if he gave his son who is a worship leader, a very amazing guitar that as a father he would be sad if Brian sold it out of guilt of owning such a nice guitar and settling for a practical one. In other words when we see resource coming from a Father who loves us we won't just sell it or give it away when we are supposed to inherit it. It's like Esau giving up his inheritance for a bowl of soup, there are times we are tempted to be "Normal" or to shun God's extravagance because of other needs in our lives, or the needs of others. But if you have a relationship to God as a Father you cannot just sell your resource that He has given, or sacrifice something just so you can have help.

We do not have a "divine right" to extreme prosperity, as some have falsely taught. But neither do we need to feel guilty about the material things God provides for us. Of course we need to hold everything before God, they are His in our lives and through Him we get to steward them as sons and daughters. Paul even reminded Timothy to help people: "to be generous and ready to share," storing up treasure in heaven. But when God blesses us materially we can thankfully enjoy the things He has richly supplied (1 Tim. 6:17–19).

## OUR REWARD IS JESUS SO WE SHOULD SEE EVERY BLESSING THROUGH HIM

When Jesus is the focus of our life, that means that when provision comes we are balancing our perspective with Jesus in the center of view. Is this resource for me, for my marriage, for my family, for my church, for my city, for my business, how is this part of the story of how my life gets to bring His transformative nature to the Earth?

The Jewish people have been praying prayers about blessing since they were recited the first time. Some weekly like Numbers 6:24–26 New International Version (NIV)

> *"The Lord bless you*
> *and keep you;*
> *the Lord make his face shine on you*
> *and be gracious to you;*
> *the Lord turn his face toward you*
> *and give you peace."*

This prayer is all about receiving the expected blessing, favor, abundance, provision, social connections, and material blessings. God always set His people's identity that He would provide for them in unusual ways to show that He loves them which proves His nature to the world around them.

We see how this witnessed to the world in Solomon's life. The Queen of Sheba came to Solomon and saw all that he had built with the wisdom and abundance of God and said to him "Surely your God loves His people because He has raised up a man like you! Praise be to your God!" She worshipped Solomon's God, our God because she put herself as a leader in his role and realized there was a drastic difference in her leadership and his. She was basically saved through the comparision of God's blessing on His people that displayed His love.

## GOD PROVIDES ABUNDANTLY FOR OUR
## EMOTIONAL & SPIRITUAL NEEDS

God's ultimate goal is always spiritual provision that brings transformation and His purpose. When God brings a material, relational, business, or other types of blessing He always has a spiritual reason behind it. There are always spiritual reasons if He withholds anything from us.

God is a provider, it is one of His names. This means that He will provide abundantly for all our needs—material, emotional, and spiritual. Some of you reading this may believe that but you have never partnered your personal faith for your life for this very purpose and that is what this book is for. You may think, "That's nice poetry, to say that God provides abundantly for all my needs. But I have never seen that. He hasn't done that for me. I need provision and I am in survival mode, I'm emotionally needy. Spiritually, I don't feel close to God."

I got married late, and I had a successful single life. When I met Cherie though, I fell in love within weeks and she felt like the greatest thing out of salvation that God ever did for me. Our friendship and the way we get to process life together has changed me so many times in our marriage that I haven't stopped being grateful. I remember a prayer I had prayed after being in LA for a time: "God, I don't want to do this without my wife, my life partner. Please send me someone I can truly partner with in life, spiritual purpose, family, and fun." It was a few years later but I knew from that point she was on her way because God is a good Father and wants what I want first, then puts it in my heart so I can pray it. When she came, it was like a whirlwind and I grew so much from our relationship that other friends in my life have told me, "I like you so much better now that you are married and have kids. You were good before but you are great now." I laugh at this because that's what God providing emotionally for us does, creates a greatness that we wouldn't access if it was just us or we were self-made. We have a provider that dreamed of every relationship and resource we would ever need before we were in our mother's womb!

God provides in ways we would never expect. He plants seeds in the garden of our life, that as we read our Bible, pray, declare, and hear from Him we start to see miraculous fruit form in our circumstances and opportunities. You will notice that theme in this book of the seeds germinating and being planted, sprouting, and they represent your faith coming alive.

The Father can't help but give those who fall in love with His Son Jesus, full access to Him. Jesus is God's greatest provision to you: "For God so loved the world, that He gave His only begotten Son, that whoever believes in Him should not perish, but have eternal life" (John 3:16). All the promises of God are "Yes" in Christ (2 Cor. 1:20). He is inviting you to know Him as provider and then to become like Jesus, to provide the kingdom for those in need through your family, career, ministry, and calling.

This book is for you because it is going to help you take personal ownership over scriptures, prayers, and prophecies that are for you for now.

*We can be certain that God will give us the strength and resources we need to live through any situation in life that he ordains. The will of God will never take us where the grace of God cannot sustain us.*

—Billy Graham

*How would you live differently today if you believed deep down that God had crowned your year with his goodness? What would you dare to accomplish for his kingdom if you believed the path he has set you on drips with abundance? He has…and He will. The God we serve has purpose and plans for your life that are good. His thoughts about you are good; his will for you is good. All things are made new in His presence… your glorious future was planned before the foundations of the earth.*

—Brian Houston

*There is nothing impossible with God. All the impossibility is with us when we measure God by the limitations of our unbelief.*

—Smith Wigglesworth

# PROVISION FOR FINANCES & RESOURCES

$

*And my God will meet all your needs
according to his glorious riches in
Christ Jesus.*

**Philippians 4:19 (NIV)**

*Since he did not spare even his own Son but
gave him up for us all, won't he also give us
everything else?*

**Romans 8:32 (NLT)**

*The LORD will not let the godly go hungry,
but he refuses to satisfy the craving
of the wicked.*

**Proverbs 10:3 (NLT)**

# PROPHECY

I am a Father, and it is My good pleasure to give you My Kingdom. My Kingdom is not just principles or theory. It is tangible and requires provision in the natural. I thought of all the good works you would do before time began and I prepared a storehouse for you in Heaven that you can access by faith. Every resource you need to live the complete life I have given you is already available. My Son gave you the keys to the Kingdom, the keys to unlock these resources. They are already in your hands.

Resources to do all that I have dreamed for you to do are available. Resources of family, finances, properties, technologies, relationships, anointing, gifts, talents, they are all in My heart for you. I don't lack any imagination for what is needed, I know what you need. It was never My intention to keep you here just to survive, but to actually overcome. When you allow yourself to have the overcomer's mindset that My Son demonstrated, you will begin to access the riches of My provision so you can treasure the riches of My glory.

Everything that I have designed for you to do is so that My Son can inherit the fullness of His reward that He paid for on the cross. I will spare no expense in giving Him everything He died for. You are a powerful part of this equation. Your life of love will cause His great reward to be realized. I have given you a people to love, a tribe. They may be in your family, your neighborhood, your industry, city, or country. They may be a marginalized

**$**

group, a race, or the people behind social or environmental issues. I will give you everything you need to make My love a complete picture to them.

Just like someone with great wealth would plan their children's and grandchildren's inheritance, as well as their footprint on the world beyond their family, I am planning everything for you and with you.

If there is a revival, there are powerful resources that go into creating it: real estate and properties, finances, music, labor, media, and I have already weighed it in full, preplanning the resource as part of the purpose. If there is a business that needs to be planted, I have already seeded your life with the connections you will need to manifest its fullness. Whether it's an accountant or a sub-contractor, cry out to Me and let Me show you how vast My love for you and My Son is. If there is ingenuity or a solution needed, I have already planted the answers to huge problems in your generation and they are attainable to the humble and pure.

Finances were never supposed to rule your life. Resources were never supposed to be an oppressor over you, but I have given you the ability to overcome and powerfully steward everything I have created. You are called to be the master over the resources in your life, believing Me for everything that I put faith in you for.

If you will accept My role as Father in your life, it comes with this kind of love. You will have to know Me as a Provider and as someone who has given you the ability to produce resources.

I am leading you down powerful paths that you wouldn't have chosen for yourself. I see what needs to be developed in you so that you can steward all that I have for you, inherit My Kingdom, and bring My Son His reward. I love you and am building you up as an entrusted son to steward My Heavenly Kingdom with Me, on earth as it is in Heaven.

## PRAYER

God, I want to know You in Your nature as my Father and my Provider. I want to see You as a good Father and understand that there was never an intention of lack in my life. I pray that You would bring revelation to me of Your love for me and the world around me, and that You would use my life as a great resource center for everyone I am called to reach.

God, I have many needs, and on top of that, I have many desires. Teach me to walk with You so that these are not just my dreams, but I can see Your desires, which are greater than mine. Help me to have belief that I am called to reflect Your Father's nature and be a powerful provider on the earth to the world around me.

I pray that You would take from me any poverty mentality. I surrender any area of my thinking that has a pattern of lack and ask that You rewire it with truth. If my family generationally reproduced poverty, cut it off so that I can believe in the fullness of Your provision for my life, for my family, and for my calling.

**$**

Jesus, I want to bring You the fullness of Your reward. I pray that I would have access to every natural resource I need, without lack, so that I have the impact You designed me to walk in.

Father, I want to trust You and I choose to partner my faith with Your heart over my finances, properties, relationships, and every resource You desire for me to access. Help me to step away from unbelief and fear that hold back what You dreamed for me before I was even in my mother's womb.

God, I invite You to be my Provider, and I receive Your ability to produce resources and finances for everything You have created me for, and for everyone You have called me to love.

AMEN!

# DECLARATION

*Deuteronomy 8:18 (NIV)*

*But remember the Lord your God, for it is He who gives you the ability to produce wealth, and so confirms His covenant, which he swore to your ancestors, as it is today.*

I declare that as a Father, You have given me the ability to produce wealth and resources.

*Exodus 31:1–5 (NIV)*

*Then the Lord said to Moses, "See, I have chosen Bezalel son of Uri, the son of Hur, of the tribe of Judah, and I have filled him with the Spirit of God, with wisdom, with understanding, with knowledge and with all kinds of skills—to make artistic designs for work in gold, silver and bronze, to cut and set stones, to work in wood, and to engage in all kinds of crafts."*

I declare that You have filled me with Your Spirit, and I have access to knowledge, wisdom, understanding, revelation, and all kinds of skills to create everything with You that would bring Jesus His full reward through my life.

*Matthew 16:19 (TPT)*

*I will give you the keys of heaven's kingdom realm to forbid on earth that which is forbidden in heaven, and to release on earth that which is released in heaven.*

I declare that as the Father of the only Kingdom that will last forever, You have given me keys to this Kingdom to release every resource needed to bring Your Kingdom of Heaven to the earth. I declare that You will give me resources and finances to shut the gates of hell and forbid the work of the kingdom of darkness on the earth.

*Ephesians 3:20 (TPT)*

*Never doubt God's mighty power to work in you and accomplish all this. He will achieve infinitely more than your greatest request, your most unbelievable dream, and exceed your wildest imagination! He will outdo them all, for his miraculous power constantly energizes you.*

I declare, God, that Your power will accomplish this, not mine. I declare that Your dreams will be accomplished in my life and that Your dreams exceed anything in my wildest imagination. I declare that You will outdo what I could hope for or imagine and that You will work Your power to energize me to dream with You as Provider over my resources and finances.

AMEN!

*God is always doing 10,000 things in your life, but you may be aware of three of them.*

—John Piper

*God has the most provision for your marriage and your family, don't wait too long to create them because in them you will also find access to greater provision for every other dream.*

—Anonymous

*Wives don't need a good provider; they need a Godly man who will help them trust in the Provider.*

—Nick Vujicic

# PROVISION FOR RELATIONSHIPS & FAMILY

*For the LORD God is our sun and our shield. He gives us grace and glory. The LORD will withhold no good thing from those who do what is right.*

Psalm 84:11 (NLT)

*Once I was young, and now I am old. Yet I have never seen the godly abandoned or their children begging for bread.*

Psalm 37:25 (NLT)

*If you, imperfect as you are, know how to lovingly take care of your children and give them what's best, how much more ready is your heavenly Father to give wonderful gifts to those who ask him?*

Matthew 7:11 (TPT)

# PROPHECY

God designed you to be in His family and to be a powerful creator and reproducer of a healthy family. It is one of the greatest provisions; it is what the whole Bible is about. When the Father created you, He created you to have a healthy childhood, a wonderful single life, and a beautiful marriage. He designed you to thrive as a parent and grandparent, creating a legacy for future generations.

For every area of a broken family or relationship, God wants to come and restore you as if there never was any brokenness. He wants to give you hope and faith to not just rebuild a crumbling area, but to actually create a strong tower in areas that felt like they could never be strong.

For those of you who are single: God loves you so much and He would never want you to see yourself as incomplete. You are enough and He is your reward and treasure. He is your provision in a relationship. There is no relationship as fulfilling as a relationship with Him, and He wants to give Himself to you. Look at loneliness and longing as if they were hunger. Jesus Himself said in Matthew 5: "Blessed are the hungry for they will be filled." Don't allow your single life to feel less worthy than a married life. God has a thriving and abundant life for you now, and you can bloom in the community that you are planted.

God has also wired us for companionship and for those of you who want to one day be married, God trusts you as a husband or wife. He is building in you the everlasting quality of His love and has someone who will also reflect that back to you. He is giving you eyes to see someone past what everyone else sees. He is going to allow you to love someone with the love that says, "I know who you are before you are even there." The kind of love that calls things that are not as though they are. He is a powerful Provider of marriage and love.

For those who are already married: God has provided every tool you need to have the marriage He dreamed for you. He has tools that He will develop in you both internally and externally. He wants to make your marriage a great source of provision for the world around you. Your love is a resource center, preaching thousands of sermons that are never shared in a church service. He has given you the ability to build each other up and declare truth into each other that no other relationship was designed for. He wants to give you the ability to surrender the powerful self to someone else so that they can do life with you. He is a provider of counsel, wisdom, and growth in your marriage. He also blesses marriages with finances and resources because they were always part of His redemptive plan.

For those who are experiencing marriage difficulties: He can work even your weakness and sin for the good of your marriage if you turn to Him, if you allow Him to change you and if you turn your affection back to your spouse. God has provision for every problem. You are not alone, so don't isolate. The weakness you face is not unique, so don't allow the lie that no one will understand harden your heart and prevent you from getting help. God already has the provision of help, relationships, and tools to bring you spiritual breakthrough. He can take what would normally require years of healing and therapy, and make it happen over a condensed period of time, or even instantly, if you soften your heart and become a leader in the provision of health. He is the Provider of life.

For your children and grandchildren: God wants to make you a powerful provider for your children and grandchildren. He has given you His example and He wants to ignite faith and courage for every resource that He has provided for you. Don't look at what wasn't provided for you growing up, look at what God is saying you are capable of. For some of you reading this, He wants you to see your children and grandchildren as part of His provision for you. Some of you are afraid to have all the children He has called you to have because of fear that you lack finances or resources, but God is saying, "I always bless the increase of family with increase of provision if you are walking with Me. Don't be afraid of the blessing of a new life and how it will affect your money, time, or capacity in life. I will bring a fruitfulness to your life with each child that you would not have had if you had limited Me. You will know when to stop, but it won't be because of fear or exhaustion."

God is sending His words of encouragement and affirmation to you in areas of family. It is one of the primary places that His voice speaks and He wants to lead you and empower your choices. Trust God in your family and allow Him to be Provider, and your relationships will be a light in this generation of brokenness and darkness.

# PRAYER

God, thank you that You are the provider of community when I am single, marriage when I am ready, and children and grandchildren as a blessing to me. Thank you that You have EVERY provision for each stage of my family life and that the more it grows, the more finances, resources, and creativity to steward these roles will be available.

Let me see myself as a provider, made in Your image. I take on your provision to be a powerful builder of relationships and family. Where I have sometimes waited for others to bring resource to me or to my life and relationships, I pray that You would empower me to be a benefactor and father or mother to those in my life.

Change the narrative in my mind and heart when I feel like I am unqualified or unworthy in areas of relational love. When I face hardship in relationships and family, give me a vision of how to manage my heart and operate out of Your love. Heal fear and unbelief regarding provision and resources of relationships in my life. Take it from my mind, heart, and emotions. I can't become who You have called me to be if I am limited to my own resources and provision, but You have called me to produce more than I am able to with my own skills and talents. Help me to trust You for that. I pray that You would give me anticipation and excitement in all that You want to build in my relationships.

God, I pray that every resource of finances, properties, business, anointing, talent, skill, and education that You have for me, my spouse, my kids, my grandkids, and my relationships would be real in my spirit right now. Thank you that provision is already available and will be released as needed. Help me to know that my spiritual bank account is full of everything needed, even when my natural situation doesn't yet look that way.

I pray that You would keep me in faith so that I will partner with Your plan of provision for my life. Thank you that You have relationships on the way to help me and thank you that I am a relationship that is on the way to help others. Let my life be a provision for others as Jesus's life has been a provision for me.

AMEN

*God said, "It's not good for the Man to be alone; I'll make him a helper, a companion." So God formed from the dirt of the ground all the animals of the field and all the birds of the air. He brought them to the Man to see what he would name them. Whatever the Man called each living creature, that was its name. The Man named the cattle, named the birds of the air, named the wild animals; but he didn't find a suitable companion. God put the Man into a deep sleep. As he slept he removed one of his ribs and replaced it with flesh. God then used the rib that he had taken from the Man to make Woman and presented her to the Man.*

Genesis 2:18–22 (MSG)

# DECLARATION

I proclaim over myself and my family that we will be fully provided for by our Provider. I declare that my family will be put in order and equipped for its intended purpose by the Word of Almighty God, in the name of Jesus.

I declare that God has made me in His image for my family as a father/mother and as a provider. God has given me the ability to produce the resources and finances our family needs and we will have more than enough.

I declare that God has unlimited tools to problem solve, be creative, and educate me and my family through any hardship we face. I declare that when I ask for wisdom, He will give it to me generously (James 1).

I proclaim over myself and my family that I am committed to building a legacy, overcoming everything that has come down our generational line, and building my children and grandchildren's inheritance.

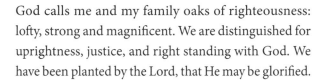

God calls me and my family oaks of righteousness: lofty, strong and magnificent. We are distinguished for uprightness, justice, and right standing with God. We have been planted by the Lord, that He may be glorified.

Declaration for broken families:

We declare that brokenness in families will come under every resource and dominion of God the Father, our Provider. God is going to take crooked and uneven relationships and make them straight and level!

We declare that our family, because Jesus IS LORD and will help us whenever we experience pain or loss, will receive consolation and joy in exchange for our mourning. God exchanges beauty for our ashes. Our family receives the garment expressive of praise in exchange for a heavy, burdened, and failing spirit.

We declare over our city and nation that the ruined families are being righteously rebuilt. Those that have been desolate are being built up. The devastated are being renewed in the way of the Lord.

We declare that the solitary will be placed in families. The Lord gives the desolate a home in which to dwell. He leads the prisoners out to prosperity. But the rebellious dwell in a parched land.

In Jesus's name, we declare healing and wholeness to those who have been used and abused by family members! In the name of Jesus, we bind up the works of the enemy and every hidden thing of darkness. We boldly declare deliverance to those who have been held captive in the cycle of abuse and domestic violence!

The peace of God rules and reigns in our households!

AMEN!

*Divine favor causes you to rise to the top in your sphere of influence, and the reality is that favor can be recognized more easily if you start at the bottom.*

– Bill Johnson

*Abundance isn't God's provision for me to live in luxury. It's His provision for me to help others live. God entrusts me with His money not to build my kingdom on earth, but to build his kingdom in heaven.*

– Randy Alcorn

*The world looks at what you have, while God sees who you have. The world's system is based on what you have done, while God looks at what Jesus has done on the cross for you.*

–Joseph Prince

# PROVISION FOR INFLUENCE, FAVOR, & SOCIAL CAPITAL

*For I know the plans and thoughts that I have for you, says the Lord, plans for peace and well-being and not for disaster, to give you a future and a hope.*

Jeremiah 29:11 (AMP)

*God will lavish you with good things: children from your womb, offspring from your animals, and crops from your land, the land that God promised your ancestors that he would give you. God will throw open the doors of his sky vaults and pour rain on your land on schedule and bless the work you take in hand. You will lend to many nations but you yourself won't have to take out a loan. God will make you the head, not the tail; you'll always be the top dog, never the bottom dog, as you obediently listen to and diligently keep the commands of God, your God, that I am commanding you today.*

Deuteronomy 28: 11–14 (MSG)

3/8/22

# PROPHECY

Before time began, I dreamed of you and how you would shine. I created you to have influence. I formed you to be loved. I formed you to carry favor. It is how you are wired, and I am developing in you the ability to shine from the highest place that you can in your lifetime.

You were made for influence. You were made to be a role model and to set a standard. My fruit in your spirit and character make you distinct. People will want to be around you, work with you, serve you, and give to you. I have called you to be a resource center, full of information, solutions, counsel, talent, gifts, and love. People will wonder how you are so full of grace. They will bless you from their own resources and influence because influence attracts and multiplies influence.

I am enlarging your sphere of influence. I'm preparing you for this great multiplication. Just like Daniel, Joseph, and Esther occupied positions of influence, they are a prototype for My influence and favor in action for you and for this generation.

I am placing favor on your life. I want to put so much love and purpose in you that you will walk into the room and people will expect greatness from you.

Even in your weakness I will show off My strength and My delight. I will use your failures to bring restoration, not only to you, but to many. Your scars will protect many, up to a whole generation, from the same pain.

Just as My Son grew in favor with man and in obedience to Me, I am growing you in favor that can create momentum in your lifetime that will cause you to live dog years. As you experience My provision of favor, you will feel an expanded and extended life of purpose, as if your time is multiplied. You will not live in "time poverty," but you will feel like you have more time because of My favor on your life and the resources that come with it.

I am going to bring you relationships with people you could have never accessed without Me. Just as when Solomon was building My temple, the greatest craftsmen came together in one generation to help him. Then kings and queens came from everywhere to see what was built. They honored him in the nations and his influence abounded so that everything he needed in order to walk in the fullness of My blessing was there. I have designed your favor to show people My love for them. Just like the Queen of Sheba came and told Solomon "Surely your God loves His people because He raised up a man like you." This is how I am creating favor in your life.

People who I have called to recognize you will not know how to relate to you except to bless you. They will give you their entire network of friends. You will be introduced way past your socioeconomic standing. You will be brought into a sphere of influence with people beyond your circle, career, influence, and own social network.

As the Provider, I brought My Son into influence, showing Him who to spend time with and how to pour His life into theirs. He went to places that no one expected, places that rabbis don't normally go. I am also bringing you into places of influence that are rare and that you wouldn't have picked for yourself. But you will delight in these places as you see them through My eyes, and they will multiply your impact.

I am your Provider of influence and favor.

# PRAYER

God, my Provider, I receive Your favor. I say yes to shining from the highest lampstand that You have planned for me to shine from. I say yes to loving people who I would normally not see in my realm of influence, as well as those who are in different areas racially, socioeconomically, geographically, those in different careers, and those across age and gender gaps. I ask You to form a "yes" in my heart to influence and favor that only comes from You. Let me not be satisfied with what I can build in my own strength and my own networking but bring me into the relational network that demonstrates Your love like Solomon did to the Queen of Sheba.

God, I ask that You would give me faith for favor and influence. Take any false humility or unworthiness from me, anything that would cause me to think I don't deserve what You are bringing me. I know that the mindset of unworthiness is a dishonor to the Cross. I receive the grace, favor, and influence that Jesus paid a price for, and that I cannot earn.

Take away pride that makes me want to build in my own strength and skill alone. Thank you that as I become interdependent on Your nature and voice that You will lead me into spheres of influence that I couldn't get to without You.

God, I embrace Your influence. I recognize that Your influence is given to reveal deeper levels of Your love and life. Help me to not settle into workaholism or complacency in my career or ministry, but keep my eyes on the prize of love: that I am not doing this just for You, I am doing it with You so that love prevails. Heal any place where I have disconnected from others. Touch my identity so that self-importance or self-reliance aren't my operating system. Heal me from exposure to bad models who demonstrated disconnected favor, influence, or fame that was for the sake of greed, idolatry, ego, or self.

Thank you, God, that I am supposed to enjoy favor and that You designed me to thrive in influence. You have called me to build social capital that has great value. Help me to use all You have given me for Your sake and benefit, giving everything away freely and with great excitement whenever it can serve Your purposes.

Protect me from being stingy with relationships, jealous with outcomes, or feeling remorse when I am not included, even when I helped create connection.

Jesus, thank you that there is always more than enough influence and favor in You. You always bless a generous heart but resist the proud. Wire me for favor, give me the most I can carry in this one life You have given me. Thank you that You have already given me an identity in Heaven that carries the highest entitlement of favor, and that I already get to influence with Heaven. Let me manifest that in the greatest way, on earth as it is in Heaven.

AMEN!

*For God's mighty miracles astound me!*
*His wonders are so delightfully mysterious*
*that they leave all who seek them astonished.*
*Everything he does is full of splendor and beauty!*
*Each miracle demonstrates his eternal perfection.*
*His unforgettable works of surpassing wonder*
*reveal his grace and tender mercy.*
*He satisfies all who love and trust him,*
*and he keeps every promise he makes.*
*He reveals mighty power and marvels to his people*
*by handing them nations as a gift.*

**Psalm 111:2–6 (TPT)**

*Those who live to bless others*
*will have blessings heaped upon them,*
*and the one who pours out his life to pour out*
*blessings will be saturated with favor.*

**Proverbs 11:25 (TPT)**

*His master replied, "Well done, good and faithful*
*servant! You have been faithful with a few things;*
*I will put you in charge of many things. Come and*
*share your master's happiness!"*

**Matthew 25:21 (NIV)**

# DECLARATION

I declare that God the Provider is lifting me up to shine from the highest place of favor and influence that my life can bring. I recognize that this favor is for His promise and I declare I will give birth to every promise God has put in my heart. I will become everything He created me to be.

I declare God's incredible blessings of favor and influence over my life. I will see an explosion of God's goodness; a sudden widespread increase. I will experience the surpassing greatness of God's favor. It will elevate me to a level higher than I ever dreamed. Explosive breakthrough is coming my way.

I declare that I am grateful for who God is as a Provider in my life and for what He's done. I will not take for granted the people, the opportunities, and the favor He has blessed me with. I commit to focus on what His favor is doing in me and for me and not on the hardships that are happening. I will thank Him for what I have and not complain about what I don't have. I will see each relationship and connection, moment of fame, or reward as a gift from God. My heart will overflow with His praise and gratitude for all of His goodness, and I will give Him glory and recognition.

I declare a legacy of faith over my life. I declare that I will store up blessings for future generations. My life is marked by His excellence and character because I'm making right choices and taking steps of faith. Others will want to follow me, and I will have new influence that will create God's opportunities to love well.

I declare that part of God's provision is that He will work out every detail to my advantage. In His perfect timing, everything will turn out right. I proclaim that even when it looks the opposite, I will stand in faith and know He can turn anything around instantly and that I will fulfill my destiny.

I declare that unexpected blessings are coming my way. I will move forward from barely making it in some areas, to having more than enough. The Provider will open up supernatural doors for me. He will speak to the right people about me. His blessings will chase me down and overtake me. I will be in the right place at the right time. People will go out of their way to be good to me. I am surrounded by God's favor.

I declare breakthroughs are coming in my life, sudden bursts of God's goodness. It is not a trickle, not a stream, but a flood of God's power, a flood of wisdom, a flood of favor. I am not only going to receive this but I declare I will be a provider for others. Through my obedience, I will be a provider of breakthrough. I choose to live with a mindset of breakthrough; I am expecting God to overwhelm me with His goodness and amaze me with His favor.

I declare God's supernatural favor over my life. What I could not make happen on my own, God will make happen for me.

AMEN!

*A God wise enough to create me and the world I live in is wise enough to watch out for me.*

—Philip Yancey

*Satan is a killer; his diseases are the destroyers of life. His sicknesses are the thieves of happiness, health, money, time, and effort. Christ came to give us abundant life in our spirits and in our bodies.*

—T. L. Osborn

*Miracles come out of rest. Resting in knowing who we are. It's who we are that defines us, not what we do. If we allow what we do to define who we are, then we are heading for trouble. Miracles are not done for identity; they are because of our identity.*

—Chris Gore

# PROVISION FOR HEALTH

*Beloved friend, I pray that you are prospering in every way and that you continually enjoy good health, just as your soul is prospering.*

**3 John 1:2 (TPT)**

*"He himself bore our sins" in his body on the cross, so that we might die to sins and live for righteousness; "by his wounds you have been healed."*

**1 Peter 2:24 (NIV)**

*Behold, I will bring to it health and healing, and I will heal them and reveal to them abundance of prosperity and security.*

**Jeremiah 33:6 (ESV)**

*But he was wounded for our transgressions; he was crushed for our iniquities; upon him was the chastisement that brought us peace, and with his stripes we are healed.*

**Isaiah 53:5 (ESV)**

# PROPHECY

As your Provider, I have provided you with time and health. Your days are one of My greatest resources that I have given you. When I planned you and then formed you in your mother's womb, I designed you to have everything you would need in your body; health, mind, and strength to walk out the full potential of your calling so that you could love in the fullest way.

My desire was never birth defects, handicaps, diseases, or sickness. My original plan for everyone I created was fullness of health. Suffering can be a tool to build authority, but suffering was never My intended story for you. Through Jesus, I have planted a vision in your heart of how I intended you to be at this stage in your life. I want to give you courage to believe your fullness of health, mental health, and healthy living that you are called to right now. Whether you need a miraculous breakthrough for this to manifest, or a new healthy living plan, I want to walk with you.

Just like a billionaire wouldn't spare any expense if his child were dying of a rare disease, I spared no expense for you. I gave up My most precious resource on your behalf. I gave My Son, Jesus, and He died so that you can get everything that I promised for your life.

Look at My heart, I want you to be healthy even more than you do. Just as a natural father would take away the suffering of their child if they could, I sent My Son to take away your suffering. Jesus paid a price on the cross and released healing as part of the resurrection. My Spirit brings you into wisdom, health, and well-being when you partner your faith to Me. I have given you a sound mind. I have given you power over sickness and disease.

I want to use the natural and the spiritual to bring increase to your health. I want to give you a vision of what your health should be, and I want to give you the zeal to work towards that vision.

Don't settle for less or give up on your health journey, unless you are walking in fullness and you can do everything I have called you to. But if you are lacking, ask Me for every resource that you need, and look for My provision. I would never leave you stuck but will use everything for your good to serve My story in your life.

My book of life has so much already written about you, and none of it says "Sickness, disease, handicap, or mental disability." Let My love manifest healing in you and release to you the ability to manage suffering. Let My Spirit bring you wisdom about your wellness and health. I want you to live fully for all the days I intended for you. Ask Me for help, don't grow complacent and settle into sickness. It is not part of My story for you. It is not your permanent condition. Let Heaven and My everlasting life dwell in you, and let that motivate you when you are suffering or afflicted.

# PRAYER & DECLARATIONS

God, give me Your plans and wisdom so I can live as the healthiest version of myself for all the days I have on this side of eternity. Give me wisdom about exercise, food, sleep, water consumption, boundaries, margins of time, and relationships. Let me not feel overwhelmed by my health/work/life balance. Instead, I embrace my identity in You as someone who builds and works toward health.

For those who are healthy and pursuing more health: Thank you that You are my Provider and care so much about my body, mind, and emotional health. Help me look at food the way You intended it. Give me the desire to choose foods that bring energy and vitality to my body and clarity to my mind. God, provide me with Your exercise plan for my life. Give me enthusiasm to exercise so that I may strengthen my body and have the energy to do the things I need to do. Help me to live in the right work/ life balance so that I can honor the time You have given me.

For those who are sick, in chronic pain, or who have a disease: Thank you for my life, my body, and my health. I pray that You would manifest Your original design in my body at this very stage in my life. Let my body reflect Your will, let every cell respond to Your love. I pray Your full provision of health over my body. Whatever vehicle of healing You have for me, God, I invite You to bring it into my life. I choose to partner with You when I am sick, and to seek prayer first. I also commit to not isolate, but to get medical help and to share the burden of my issue with someone I love, because I know that their empathy and compassion is part of Your provision in my life.

On days when my hope is weak and my will is tired, I pray that You would be my inner strength to keep pressing in. Let me not commit the sin of independence and resist prayer or medical attention, but rather, help me to actively partner faith with Your provision of health for my life. I choose to keep moving forward and to not lie down in my bed of sickness. I know You will provide connections. Help me to keep an open heart of communication with my community so that if there is a key connection for healing or health I will find it. Help me pursue every provision You have for my healing. Even when something I have tried doesn't work out, give me the bold faith to try again, or try other options. Give me faith and strength to battle and not submit to this health condition. Thank you that everlasting health is my story and this current issue has a limited amount of days.

For those who have a handicap or disability: Thank you, God, that You are my Provider. Thank you for both supernatural healing and for wise management of what I have. Thank you that I am not defined by what I lack, and for however long I carry this affliction in my body or neurology, it does not separate me from Your love or who You have called me to be. Thank you for creative solutions that You are resourcing me with so that I can live in fullness. Thank you for technologies, medical processes, finances, and resources that You are bringing to help me in life. Your desire is for me to never be spiritually hindered by this disability. God, help me walk in Your character and compassion toward those who sometimes misunderstand me. Help me to be a vehicle of love and grace to everyone around me. Thank you, Jesus, for modeling to me a life that was misunderstood many times and, yet, still thrived. Thank you for giving me a model for handling rejection and pain. Thank you that You showed, even in Your own weakness, that Your Father was strong. Now I know I can do all things through You, Jesus. Thank you for a plan of health and that I can also experience Your miracle-working power. Give me vision for Your power. Let me envision my body in the fullness of the provision You have for me here on the earth.

For those who have mental disabilities or illness: God, my Provider, I thank you that one of the promises You have given me is a sound and powerful mind. I pray that You would touch my mind and renew it, rewire it, and heal it so that I can be completely connected to You, myself, and the world around me. I thank you that You created me to think powerfully, that You control the chemical balance in my body, that You created the intellect, that You stimulate the neuropathways. I give You my mind and I ask You to give me the strength to receive every provision You have for me. Whether it is spiritual prayer, counseling, medicine, training, or therapy, help me to be brave and have faith to walk in Your fullness in this area. God, thank you that even in the midst of this weakness, You still can work everything for my good. I pray that You would give me the mental stamina and strength to constantly progress and not stagnate in this area. Let me not accept status quo and the label of disability or mental condition. Show me Your provision and give me faith to apprehend every aspect of it. Help me to celebrate the breakthroughs. Thank you for using me to love people and that in my weakness You are strong. I pray that You would send people around me who would help pull out the best in me and that I would be a powerful contributor to my community of friends and family. Thank you that You want to provide a supernatural miracle for me and that You want my healing and wholeness more than I do. As my Provider, You already planned it for me.

AMEN!

*Stop waiting for what you want and start working what you have. This can turn your greatest frustration into your greatest potential innovation. If you'll do your part, God will begin to do what only He can do: He'll make your box bigger.*

—Steven Furtick

*Destiny is not for the comfort seekers. Destiny is for the daring and determined who are willing to endure some discomfort, delay gratification, and go where destiny leads.*

—T. D. Jakes

*Nothing is impossible. The word itself says "I'm possible."*

—Unknown

*Every great dream begins with a dreamer. Always remember, you have within you the strength, the patience, and the passion to reach for the stars to change the world.*

—Harriet Tubman

# PROVISION FOR CREATIVITY, INGENUITY, & INVENTIONS

*God can pour on the blessings in astonishing ways so that you're ready for anything and everything, more than just ready to do what needs to be done. As one psalmist puts it, He throws caution to the winds, giving to the needy in reckless abandon. His right-living, right-giving ways never run out, never wear out. This most generous God who gives seed to the farmer that becomes bread for your meals is more than extravagant with you. He gives you something you can then give away, which grows into full-formed lives, robust in God, wealthy in every way, so that you can be generous in every way, producing with us great praise to God.*

**2 Corinthians 9:8–11 (MSG)**

*Let the favor of the Lord our God be upon us and establish the work of our hands upon us; yes, establish the work of our hands!*

**Psalm 90:17 (ESV)**

# PROPHECY

Just like the first time I breathed My Spirit back into man in Exodus—for creativity, ingenuity and inventions—I also have breathed My Spirit into you. Part of knowing Me as your Provider is to know Me as a Creator. I make all things new. I have never stopped creating and am going to include this part of My nature in you, over and over again. This will allow you a rare view of life through the lens of faith—knowing that there is always a solution, invention, or creativity that can solve your problems and bring more of My Kingdom to your life and to those around you.

In your mind, the world's problems are always solvable because you have My creative power. When things feel locked, I have given you keys that the greatest finances can't open. I am bringing the power of creativity to solve problems that have stumped the smartest and most brilliant minds.

I am a creative Provider and I have creativity for your family, for your career, for your rest. I want to give you a rhythm of walking in My Spirit of creativity in your life. I have released inside of you the nature of a creator. Even if it doesn't manifest in creative talents, it will manifest in creative living. I have given you an imagination and a dream center in your spirit. Part of My provision for you is an ability to tap into hope: to dream of what I have for you, to imagine what I can do with your life. I have possibilities that will never appear until you look for Me.

I am giving you creativity, ingenuity, and inventiveness that will be a signpost in your life that causes people to wonder. They will see Me and My love as you release breakthroughs in ideas, industries, and people groups.

I am releasing the ability to produce wealth and finances. I have resources hidden in the earth that will last until the end of the age. I have resources in outer space that have untapped potential. I have built ingenuity and inventiveness inside of you so you can tap into ideas that will transform and revolutionize everything. The world will say, "We are almost out of a resource!" because they don't know Me as Provider like you do. As a good Father, I have created everything in this age to last until we are together again. I will raise up my people as stewards who will help to bring a course correction right when it is needed, so that the depletion of what I have put on the earth will be replenished within the environment. I am a good Provider.

I am anointing you to create everything that is needed for My Son, Jesus, to get His reward. Just like Bezalel, you are prepared, and I am filling you with skill, talent, and the finest craftsmanship that the world will know in areas that I am calling you to shine.

I have inventions that I have set apart for you to discover. I have solutions to problems, advancements to humanity, inventions that can heal land, food, nature, and weather. I have technology to heal the air, to advance connectivity, to change the capacity of the world to travel, to create more with less. Dream with Me about the way cities will be built in the future, the way the ecosystem will look as I release new ideas and practices that can change a whole generation. Some people will misunderstand and think that I am going to let you reap everything you have sown in humanity. But as your Provider, I cut off this curse of reaping and, as you turn your heart to Me, you will cause your land to be healed and for science to advance.

Things that would take a hundred years to invent and twenty years for society to adopt are going to be assimilated over a short period. I have cures for diseases, inventions for security, even systems of administration for governments that can change everything in a day.

I am your Father who provides, call to Me and I will show you things you would have never known. These are real things that have real implications and they will be reported about openly to the whole world, who may deny Me, but will not be able to deny the benefit that I provided through your partnership with Me. Through you, the world will know My nature as a Provider and see Me in creative ways where I would not be visible if it was not for you partnering with Me.

# PRAYER

Father and Provider, I ask You to breathe Your creativity into me. Let me create in fullness, just as You do. I repent if I have not viewed myself as a creative person. Heal my lack of creativity and fill me with faith that I will bring ingenuity, creativity, and even inventions to the world. Help me to see what is not yet as though it is, especially in areas of industry, church, agriculture, technology, or politics. Give me vision for areas that I am called to that I am not creative enough to imagine on my own.

God, I ask for the provision of natural creativity and inventions. I pray that You would speak to me and give me a new heart, a creative heart that obeys what I hear/see and have intuition about.

I ask for ingenuity for things that have been built. Let me help to advance and reinforce what You have released in previous generations that is still relevant today. Help me to bring forth advancements so the things already built fit well and are fashioned for this generation. Give me the power to innovate and bring resource to make things better according to Your divine design for today.

I ask for repair and recovery for systems that have been wrongly created. Help me to bring Your provision over science, agriculture, government, media, entertainment, medical industries, engineering, city planning, and every area that is within Your Kingdom.

Father, thank you for making me in Your image as Creator.

AMEN!

*Every gift God freely gives us is good and perfect, streaming down from the Father of lights, who shines from the heavens with no hidden shadow or darkness and is never subject to change. God was delighted to give us birth by the truth of his infallible Word so that we would fulfill his chosen destiny for us and become the favorite ones out of all his creation!*

**James 1:17–18 (TPT)**

# DECLARATION

I declare that God the Creator has made me a co-creator and is filling me with His provision of creativity, ingenuity, innovation, and advancement.

I declare that He has breathed His Spirit in me to create everything that is needed in our generation to bring Him glory. He has filled me with talents, skills, ideas, design, engineering, creative vision, and is breathing a fresh creativity into me for these areas even now.

*+ strategy*

I proclaim that God is providing management for my projects, creativity, and innovation. He is giving me administration, legal processes, patents, teams, co-workers, inventions or help for my inventions, and all that is needed to bring forth what is inside of me and manifest its fullest expression in my lifetime and beyond.

I declare that I will dream with God, and entertain the impossible in my spirit and imagination, so that I can live with a God-sized dream (Ephesians 3:20).

I declare that I will provide solutions to problems, advancement to industries, ingenuity for older industries and efforts, and creativity that hasn't been seen before

I embrace the Provider and I declare that I do not need someone to be my benefactor. Through what I am building I will be a benefactor as God has given me the ability to produce every resource needed in every area of my destiny.

AMEN!

*A firm faith in the universal providence of God is the solution of all earthly troubles.*

—B. B. Warfield

*They called me trailer trash, But our God's in the recycling business. Champions have the courage to keep turning the page because they know a better chapter lies ahead.*

—Paula White

*When we lose one blessing, another is often most unexpectedly given in its place [if we anticipate and look for it, rather than wallow in our 'supposed loss.' It can be helpful to think of the loss of that blessing as simply necessary to make way for another different blessing].*

—C. S. Lewis

# PROVISION FOR RESTORATION & REDEMPTION

*The thief comes to steal kill and destroy but I have come to give you life and life abundantly.*

John 10:10

*I have told you these things, so that in me you may have peace. In this world you will have trouble. But take heart! I have overcome the world.*

John 16:33 (NIV)

*I lift up my eyes to the mountains—where does my help come from? My help comes from the LORD, the Maker of heaven and earth.*

Psalm 121:1–2 (NIV)

*Don't be pulled in different directions or worried about a thing. Be saturated in prayer throughout each day, offering your faith-filled requests before God with overflowing gratitude. Tell him every detail of your life, then God's wonderful peace that transcends human understanding, will make the answers known to you through Jesus Christ.*

Philippians 4:6–7 (TPT)

# PROPHECY

The Father, as Provider, sent Jesus to restore all things. He knows your loss deeper than anyone. He is going to restore to you more than what was lost. You may have lost family, friends, significance, identity, or it may have been something more practical like a contract, business, property, legal case, inheritance, award, or any of number of things, but God is the God of redemption. This means He can restore you as if you never had a loss. He can also recreate another opportunity that will satisfy the desire that He has placed in your heart.

Whatever the situation of loss, lay it out in detail to Him and give His Spirit the opportunity to reveal the Father as your Provider. He will listen to your troubles carefully and with a compassionate heart and show you how He is at work in the world around you, while also at work inside of you, building trust, faith, and your ability to hear Him.

He has specific directions to lead you into. He is a good shepherd; He will lead you to good pastures—opportunities filled with life.

Whatever the enemy meant for evil God will use to serve you. The enemy not only loses—and love wins—but you will know God in a much deeper way. He will do miraculous things for you to fix the problems and bring you into His full plan.

When you lose money, a resource, or a relationship, and, in humility, turn to Him as Provider, He instantly creates a plan of restoration. Even when you can't see Him at work, angels are being dispatched to fight for you and to bring about His Kingdom on earth as it is in Heaven.

God the Provider knows how to restore. It is part of His love nature. As you get to know Him in this place of need, you will develop a faith that is so rooted and grounded that even when the worst shakings happen around you, you will not be shaken.

# PRAYER

God my Provider, come and bring Your redemptive plan to my life. As You do, heal my heart from the pain of suffering that came with my loss. Whether it was relational loss, lost money and resources, failed projects, stolen money or goods, bankruptcy, medical debt, or anything that was stolen by the enemy, I pray that You would commission Heaven to gather resources and provision in each area I have experienced loss. I agree with what Jesus said in John 10:10 and I receive Your abundant life.

I thank you, Father, that You will restore not just some, but *all* that was lost. I pray that You would create a new heart in me so that I can have faith again, especially because things are always different the next time around. Help me embrace change and be comforted by Your restoration, not comparing it to the past. Renew my mind so that I can be planted in Kingdom thoughts.

I pray an end to any trauma, negative or cyclical patterns, painful thinking, or negativity that keep my mind and heart in pain. I surrender my pain and suffering to You. I surrender betrayal, rejection, failure, undeserved attacks, and I ask that You renew and transform my mind. Renew my Spirit where I feel jaded or nervous. I embrace Your words over my life to experience a peace that passes all understanding.

Help my soul to trust in You and trust the people You bring into my life. Help me to trust my own ability to hear Your voice. I know You are bringing fresh relationships, resources, and provisions; help me to trust them as they come and exchange doubt for faith with each restoration that You bring. Heal my unbelief as You renew me and my life.

I choose to stand in faith in Your nature as Provider, and I ask You to bring fullness of provision in this area of loss. Thank you, Jesus, that what the enemy meant for evil, You will use to serve me. Thank you that I am going to experience blessing and provisions in this area and be strong once again. Thank you that I get to know You in a deeper way because of these circumstances and that You are near to those who have experienced loss.

AMEN!

# DECLARATION

I thank you, God, my Provider, for Your plan of divine restoration. Thank you that Your Word and Your love for me never fails.

I declare the blood of Jesus Christ to cleanse me and my family from any kind of sin that may have opened doors to allow the enemy to steal from me in any way. I ask God to show me areas of my life that need to grow or change.

I pray, Oh LORD, just as You enabled David and his men to recover all that was stolen from them, I ask that You empower me and my family by Your Spirit to recover everything that has been stolen from us in the past, in Jesus' name.

I declare that the Holy Spirit will show me what to do to manifest the full recovery plan of the LORD.

I declare that I am baptized with grace for all-around victory over the works of darkness this year, in Jesus's name.

I pray and decree that from now on, nothing belonging to me, my family, or my ministry shall be missing, in Jesus's name.

I declare that in every area in the past where I have experienced shame, I receive a double restoration, according to Your Word, in Jesus's name.

I declare a total restoration for all the years that feel like they were not fruitful or when I made bad choices. As I turn to You, Provider, I ask for You to restore my life and time as if I had never wasted it.

I declare restoration in my health, finances, family, ministry, children, and business, in Jesus's name!

AMEN!

*It's what you sow that multiplies, not what you keep in the barn.*

—Adrian Rogers

*God wants us to prosper financially, to have plenty of money, to fulfill the destiny He has laid out for us.*

—Joel Osteen

*God is raising up individuals who will carry the full manifestation of his desire. These people will take a leap of faith, in the hope that everything they invest into will prosper and with the goal of delivering to Jesus his great reward.*

—Shawn Bolz,
*Keys to Heaven's Economy:
An Angelic Visitation from the Minister of Finance*

$

# PROVISION FOR WEALTH CREATION & ABUNDANCE

*You shall remember the Lord your God, for it is he who gives you power to get wealth, that he may confirm his covenant that he swore to your fathers, as it is this day.*

Deuteronomy 8:18 (ESV)

*Remember this: Whoever sows sparingly will also reap sparingly, and whoever sows generously will also reap generously. Each of you should give what you have decided in your heart to give, not reluctantly or under compulsion, for God loves a cheerful giver. And God is able to bless you abundantly, so that in all things at all times, having all that you need, you will abound in every good work.*

2 Corinthians 9:6–8 (NIV)

*Command those who are rich in this present world not to be arrogant nor to put their hope in wealth, which is so uncertain, but to put their hope in God, who richly provides us with everything for our enjoyment.*

1 Timothy 6:17 (NIV)

# PROPHECY

God has spoken all through the Scriptures about blessing, prosperity, wealth, and abundance. He has finances for every project, business, family, and purpose. He would never give you the purpose without pouring out the resource. He wants to train you to reign, which is your eternal position.

I had a vision of the river of God in the book of Revelation. It has trees planted by it that are always in season, they bear fruit twelve times a year. The river itself is teeming with life and as clear as crystal. It is a picture of our eternity with God; there is fullness. He wants to provide clarity to you. He wants to provide fruit in all seasons. He wants to provide healing all the time. He wants to provide abundant life in you and around you. He put Adam and Eve in the garden to tend and steward it from the beginning because that is who they were supposed to be: managers of the abundance of God's creation.

Ezekiel saw this river as well, and he prophesied about it. He used all the same imagery, but he also talked about entering the river. The more faith he had, the deeper he went, until it was over his head. He was speaking about the blessing of God that will overtake His people if they enter the river. He also saw the river draining all the way to the Dead Sea, which is the lowest sea in the world with no outlet. It is dead with salt. Ezekiel saw the living river running and purifying the dead river. As you lean into God's provision, industries, businesses, and world systems that have died or that are not a source of life, it will be redeemed and become teeming with God's abundant life.

Jesus saw this river and said it springs up from within our own belly. He shared the parable in John 7:38 because He knew you would be the temple that God has chosen for His Spirit to dwell in. His river comes from His work within you.

God has called you to step into the river. He has provided tools inside of you, opportunities outside of you, and prophetic insight to help you create wealth and resources.

He has dates already marked on your calendar for divine appointments that will make history in your life.

He will bring you into opportunities that make sense, but also opportunities that you would have never pursued or imagined or even felt qualified for or interested in. But you will know these opportunities are from Him.

He wants to multiply your capacity to create resources with Him. For many, as a Provider, He has multiple streams of income per household and you are not stuck with just one opportunity.

Imagine if your natural father was the richest man in the world right now. What if he was presented with the best investment and business opportunities, but he only revealed to you one little business that created mediocrity in comparison to his vast world of wealth? What kind of father would do that to a willing child? Your Father owns all the cattle on a thousand hills and He wants to sow resource into your life. Like the parable of the talents, as you are faithful to create resource, He will multiply your efforts in ways you couldn't even expect.

The hyper-wealthy just want to be wealthy for the comfort and the pride of life. God the Father is giving you the desire to steward all the resources you can so that you can bring Him a great reward at the end of the age. He wants to entrust you because He knows you want to change lives, help the hurting and broken, touch the poor, see cities built, labor over transformation, change industries, and build ministries that transform the earth with His goodness.

How can He resist the heart He put within you?

He loves your love for His Son, Jesus, and He wants to promote you because of it. That promotion will come in the form of stewardship. That stewardship is going to bring responsibility over resources and finances.

For some of you, it is time to come out of poverty. It is time to come out of survival. It is time to come out of disparity. It is time to come into an overcomer mindset. For others who already have a measure of wealth and resource, just like in the parable of the talents, the Good Master, our God and Provider, always multiplies what is multiplied. He is going to bring you a greater measure. He will give you the talents of those who buried them in the ground.

He is calling you into breakthrough provision—provision that can become a river of blessing to others. I see you in the river, and it's time to get over your head in the abundance of God and heal every Dead Sea in this world that you are called to aim your love at.

# PRAYER

God, Provider, give me every resource that I can carry so I can create wealth and provide for others. You call me a child who is worthy of Your abundance both in eternity but also here. You are entrusting me with resources that can change nations, heal poverty, and transform industries, cities, neighborhoods, and families.

I invite Your living river to come into me from Your throne, from my intimacy with You. Speak to me about Your heart for nations. Speak to me about Your heart for my generation. Share Your secrets about the ones You love and how You want to reveal Yourself—in the greatest way in history—and You will spare no resource to do it.

Jesus, I invite Your living river to flow out of the place You are enthroned within my spirit. I pray that the river that comes out of my calling and destiny brings fruitfulness in every season. I ask that You fill my time with Your abundance, my relationships with Your new life, and my finances and resources with everything You need me to apprehend for Your glory.

Heal me of any negative relationship I have with wealth, prosperity, or abundance. If those have become a trigger to my heart, touch me and free me from anything that is false. If I have had ego regarding the provision You have already provided, or a wrong love of money, convict my heart. Teach me that Your provision is not about me, it's about You and Your love. Help me to be sacrificial in the midst of wisdom. Give me opportunities to sow resources, give extravagantly, and help others succeed as I lay down my life and serve them.

God, my Father, my Provider, I want to partner with You in Your plan to resource the earth. I want to thrive in You, and I know this will bring blessing. Help me to never repent of Your provision or blessing in my life. Help me to never have false humility when You answer my prayers with real answers that have tangible results. Help me to glory in You and not the provision. Help my heart to stay steadfast even when it is challenged more by Your goodness than it was by loss or suffering.

Train me in the ways of abundance. Teach me in the ways of wealth creation. Disciple my inner man to be a firm foundation of faith for Your abundance in all the areas You are calling me into. In Your beautiful name and nature, I pray.

AMEN!

*Jesus shouted to them, "Throw your net over the starboard side, and you'll catch some!" And so they did as he said, and they caught so many fish they couldn't even pull in the net!*

**Proverbs 21:6 (TPT)**

*The blessing of the Lord makes rich, and he adds no sorrow with it.*

**Proverbs 10:22 (ESV)**

# DECLARATION

Father, my Provider, You have changed my thinking towards wealth. You have shifted my mindset and the mindsets of those who walk with me. We have a Kingdom perspective of giving, receiving, wealth, riches, and prosperity.

I declare that my financial status has changed; God has given me an ability over wealth creation (Deuteronomy 8:18).

I receive the secrets to wealth and prosperity. My businesses and my finances are shielded from all evil in the name of Jesus. I am walking in boldness to possess everything inherited and promised to me and my bloodline in the Word of God.

I declare that just as God blessed Sarah's womb with promise, He has impregnated me with the promise of provision, and I declare I shall not abort. I will go full-term and birth the blessings of God, which will manifest in my bloodline, in my lifetime, and even NOW!

$

I declare that I am the child of the Great Provider; therefore, I am His heir, fellow heir with Christ, sharing His inheritance with Him. Not only does the earth and everything in it belong to Jesus, it also belongs to me and my bloodline as part of our divine inheritance (Psalm 24:1; Psalm 115:16).

I declare that God can trust me with wealth and resources. I claim, command, and seize my ability to produce resources now, in the name of Jesus.

All nations will call me blessed, and I will be a delightful land (Malachi 3:12).

My gates are open continually so that the forces (wealth) of the nations can come into my life (Isaiah 60:11).

I am the righteous of Christ and now is the time for the wealth that has been stored up for me to be released in the name of Jesus.

I give, and it is given to me—good measure, pressed down, shaken together, and running over (Luke 6:38).

I commit to give freely, and I know that it will cause me to gain even more. I decree and declare I am a generous person. I will prosper, for I will pour into others and I will be poured into (Proverb 11:24–25).

The Lord teaches me to profit and leads me in the way I should go (Isaiah 48:17).

I believe the prophets, and I prosper (2 Chronicles 20:20).

I declare that every hole in my bag be closed in the name of Jesus (Haggai 1:6).

I declare my season of supernatural increase is here.

I live in the prosperity of the King (Jeremiah 23:5).

*God's path will never lack
God's provision.*

—Toby Mac

*In receiving provision from God, it
helps create in you the attitude of
a provider and it helps you stay in
gratitude. To whom is given much,
much is required.*

—John Maxwell

*God's strength behind you, His concern
for you, His love within you, and
His arms beneath you are more than
sufficient for the job ahead of you.*

—William Arthur Ward

# PROVISION FOR
# BUSINESS & CAREER

*He will give the rain for your land in its season, the early rain and the later rain, that you may gather in your grain and your wine and your oil.*

**Deuteronomy 11:14 (ESV)**

*Ask, and the gift is yours. Seek, and you'll discover. Knock, and the door will be opened for you. For every persistent one will get what he asks for. Every persistent seeker will discover what he longs for. And everyone who knocks persistently will one day find an open door.*

**Matthew 7:7–8 (TPT)**

*The plans of the diligent lead surely to abundance, but everyone who is hasty comes only to poverty.*

**Proverbs 21:5 (ESV)**

*Before you do anything, put your trust totally in God and not in yourself. Then every plan you make will succeed.*

**Proverbs 16: 3 (TPT)**

# PROPHECY

God spent millions of years dreaming of you. He prepared for you before He even spoke you into existence. The Bible says that before time began, He prepared you for good works. What you do is supposed to be an extension of who you are.

God is a Father, and as a Father He wants to nurture your identity as His child. He wants to plant seeds out of this identity that lead you to know what areas of career and business would bring you life. You will spend much of your life working, but He wants to create meaning out of the work of your hands. Not only what you do, but who you do it with are an important part of who He created you to be.

He created opportunities for where and how you would work, as well as who you would work with. He has handcrafted a plan for your life and is always moving in the atmosphere around you to stir up the potential for all that He planned.

He has created you to be the most amazing counterpart to Himself, and He will entrust you with authority in your industry and field—both to influence others in your workspace and to bring transformation beyond your working goals.

God is the Provider for business owners and those who are self-employed. He wants to provide everything you need to create a culture around you that will be just as important as the career path and marketplace you serve. He is giving you powerful tools to create resources. Part of His provision over you is that you will succeed in many ways, not just monetarily. He is making you a provider as well. You will provide contracts, sales opportunities, employment opportunities, leadership development, coaching, and family to people who would not otherwise be exposed to the atmosphere that He wants to create through you.

God is the Provider for people of influence, management, or leadership in their career. God is giving you His Father's heart to manage with wisdom and influence not just in your role, but also over the culture of the entire company. He is giving you the ability to make complicated problems seem simple, to help navigate relationships that can often be difficult, and to help in the midst of transition or change. One of the provisions God has given you is the ability to adapt and change and to create a willingness in others to adapt and change. God has put tools inside of you that will help your organization succeed. You are an integral part of your organization, and God is going to have you serve like a Joseph, Esther, or Daniel—those who held the favor of God and prospered even unrighteous countries that they were called to serve.

God is the Provider for employees of any kind. God is providing the ability to make you a skilled worker. He wants to give you a relational grace, talent beyond your years, and skill that can't be taught. He wants to advance you, provide for you, and show you your work is your mission field. He wants to anoint you for your job and anoint the job for you. God is your Provider and wants to give you an incredible experience no matter how menial the task. He is with you and considers your work worship when you dedicate it to Him. He will show you ways to prosper that no one else sees and provide help to you that seems unavailable to others.

# PRAYER

My Provider, I place my career in Your hands again and ask You to allow me to be Your partner. Speak deeply into my spirit and equip me with revelation to navigate in my industry. Give me wisdom in the marketplace. I need to have Your spiritual insight.

Help me prosper, provide the best opportunities available in my life. Assign me to my position so it is not just work and something I do, but it becomes a mission field, a spiritual occupation, and a way to transform the world around me. I know that You created me for good works from before time began. I pray that what I do in my career would align with Your original purpose for me.

God, give me Your significance even when what I am working on seems normal or mundane. I commit to work as an act of worship that is surrendered to You. I know I will bear fruit because of that.

God, I know that the enemy falsely believes that he is the owner of this world and he raises an antichrist spirit to try and control markets. Hide me from the enemy and fight for me when he comes near. Show Your enemies Your authority through the accumulation of power, favor, and transformation that comes through my career. Thank you that no weapon formed against me will prosper, but they will all lay broken at Your feet.

Holy Spirit, be my GPS in my career. Walk with me and teach me. Be a better coach than if I had the top business coach. Share Your wisdom with me and help me to wrap it around my decisions and reasoning as if it were my uniform. I commit to read the Word, to soak in it and apply it to my career, my life, and my finances.

I pray that You would keep me growing in spiritual hunger for the Bible as I pursue You in my career. Let it create a firm foundation for my feet each day I read it, and help me to miss it when I don't prioritize it.

Whether I am a business owner, entrepreneur, trade worker, artist, nurse, or am part of a private practice—no matter what You have called me to—anoint me for it. Thank you for Your process of provision, which leads me in ways I would not go myself. Thank you that I cannot be self-made or just go with my talent and skill, because You have given me a hunger to have a spiritual impact with my life and work, not just a natural one. Help me to have patience and endurance and loyalty as I walk through Your process to see the fulfillment of Your promises in my life.

God, my Provider, lead me in the marketplace and let me hear Your voice for my industry and the people who work with me so that I can be a light and voice for Your love.

AMEN!

# DECLARATION

Jesus, my Provider, I thank you that every good and perfect gift comes from You. You have promised that, if I commit whatever I do to You, then You will cause my plans to succeed. I declare that my success will come from aligning my plans with Your will. Let me hear Your voice clearly as You give me wisdom and guidance. Remind me that success is not found in the world but is found in You. May You, the Lord of all, give me success at all times and in every way.

I declare that You are assigning me to my work and giving me the anointing and power to produce Kingdom fruit. The Bible says that if I walk in Your ways and observe Your commands, I will prosper in all I do and wherever I go. Give me assurance that, as I seek Your will, You will bless me with prosperity.

Father, I declare with Deuteronomy 8:18 that it is You who gives me the ability to produce wealth. My career is Yours and I commit it into Your hands, Jesus. I know that You are the provider of success and prosperity. I declare I have the strength to resist the temptations that come with resources and wealth and, instead, glorify You in every aspect of my business.

I declare that You will bless all the work of my hands and cause me to prosper. My work will glorify You.

I declare that I will walk in Your plans and purpose for me, plans to prosper me not to harm me. I trust You with my business and career. I declare that I will work with thankfulness in my heart to You, my Provider of opportunities.

I proclaim that You are watching over my business, protecting me from danger, and leading me on the path to prosperity and success. As I am rooted and grounded in love, You are giving me all the strength I need to know the love of Christ that surpasses knowledge. I declare Your promise that I do not need to be anxious about anything, but in every situation I should present my requests to God. Even when I make mistakes and fail, Your love will cover my weakness and my future is secure in You. I proclaim You will work all things for my good.

I thank you that, as my Father and Provider, You will do far more abundantly than all that I ask or imagine, according to the power at work within me. Hallelujah!

*God's work done in God's way will never lack (provision).*

—Hudson Taylor

*The provision is in the promises.*

—Derek Prince

*If God said it, God can do it.*

—Christine Caine

# PROVISION FOR
# CHURCH & MINISTRY

*Fear the LORD, you his godly people, for those who fear him will have all they need. Even strong young lions sometimes go hungry, but those who trust in the LORD will lack no good thing.*

Psalm 34:9–10

*The Lord is my best friend and my shepherd. I always have more than enough.*

Psalm 23:1 (TPT)

*Everything we could ever need for life and complete devotion to God has already been deposited in us by his divine power. For all this was lavished upon us through the rich experience of knowing him who has called us by name and invited us to come to him through a glorious manifestation of his goodness.*

2 Peter 1:3 (TPT)

*For God will never give you the spirit of fear, but the Holy Spirit who gives you mighty power, love, and self-control.*

2 Timothy 1:7 (TPT)

# PROPHECY

I am ordaining a new breed of church builders and ministry leaders in this generation. I am generating new strategies, resources, and provisions that will change the face of Christianity. I am giving local churches strategies to uncover more streams of provision besides just tithes and offerings. I am giving itinerate and parachurch ministries ingenuity to achieve fullness. Many ministries will begin to plant businesses to support themselves and to give them further reach into society. I am commissioning many leaders to be engaged in areas that seemed off-limits before, like entertainment, politics, and finance.

I am going to enhance your vision. I am going to take you into an organizational anointing that will attract partners, family support, and abundant giving. I will give you pro-vision that will lead to provision. You will have such expert and clearly communicated vision from My heart that people will be attracted to the vision, but they will remain with you because you will have the application and implementation that causes people to see My love. Just like Solomon could see exactly how to design the temple, the city, his home, and the infrastructure, you will also get clear vision. Ask Me for it because it is the beginning of greater provision.

I will bring ready-made leaders to you who have been on maturing journeys for years and they will integrate into your leadership supernaturally. I will bring new believers that have talents and skills that you haven't dreamed of, who will be your sons and daughters. They will even be more gifted and talented than you, and this is My blessing. Don't compete with them, don't hold them back. Let them have anointing that is stronger than yours.

You are a provider like Me and you help make room for everything that is inside of those around you that is from Me. You welcome it even if it makes what you have look small in some way. People outgrow managers and bosses, but they don't outgrow fathers and mothers. Be a spiritual parent, and I will continue to parent you.

I am releasing mentors to you, even in your maturity, so that you can advance. In years to come, you will look back on this season as one of the greatest catalysts of hunger you have ever had. I am growing your faith to steward every resource you need to see My fullness in your ministry. You need finances, you need the right people in alignment, you need properties—sometimes to lease, sometimes to own. You need technology, you need internet and social media presence, you need media to develop around you, many of you need creative resources and provisions for your missions that can only come from Me. I am coming, they are on their way. Don't miss out because of unbelief. Don't just believe that I am good. Partner your faith in action to declare what is needed, no matter how big or ridiculous it feels. Speak it out loud to Me, let Me hear you come into agreement with what is in My heart. As you say it, you can claim a new level of ownership over it.

I am restoring the dignity of My people. Yes, some will hate you, but I am also releasing favor in so many other sectors. When I walked on the earth, My favor was more effective than My enemies were, no matter how many there were. I was able, even in the most hostile environment, to thrive in the Kingdom, and so will you. I am giving you favor so that My presence can cover the earth. People need your covering. They will thrive in My love, which rests in you, and they will begin to see you as a provider.

# PRAYER

God, my Provider, I receive Your provision for my vision. I receive Your resources to upgrade my ministry so my expectations can grow. Help me to turn away from any small-mindedness or an approach that doesn't work or is just maintenance. Let me not be in survival mode or become a person who is waiting to be rescued by someone with finances or resources. Let me see myself as a father/mother whom You trust to build resources with, a parent who can provide for many people so they can walk in their fullness.

Thank you that the Kingdom is always growing. That is my model of Your provision. I should be able to look back decade after decade and see what has grown.

Father, for the people You have called me to love and lead, I ask for everything we need in this season to come. I push my faith into Your provision. I ask that You move mountains of provision towards our ministry so that we can do everything with the same grace in which Jesus accomplished His mission.

Thank you, God, that in Acts 2, when You poured out Your Spirit, there were always enough resources and provision. People would freely sacrifice, even from their own resources, sharing generously because they were so fulfilled in their relationships and trusted where the ministry was going. Would You raise up that joyful abundance by moving on us in a new measure of Your Spirit?

Jesus, if there is anything in me that is stuck, slow to change, not growing, or settled in a wrong way, I ask that You uproot it. I invite You to work within me, Spirit of God, and I pray for mentors in my life. Let me not be the most powerful voice in my own ministry, church, or calling. I choose to share that voice, not just with people I lead, but also peers, mentors, and spiritual mothers and fathers. If I have been independent from those kinds of relationships, help me to accept Your provision of covenant relationships. Let the work that I do honor the relationships that the work is for.

God, in seasons where You are bringing provision to multiply Your impact through me, help me to enter into the right rhythm of rest and ministry/personal life balance. I pray that as my ministry grows, it would explode with new life so that it can only be managed with a plan from You. Thank you for being the Provider of the resources, and the skills to wield the resources.

Father, resource the ministry You have given me so that I can raise up a mature people who will be a beautiful bride for Jesus. As I long for His return, help me to be one who prepares His people.

AMEN!

# DECLARATION

In the name of Jesus, my Provider, I declare that our ministry has access to every natural resource we need to fulfill the calling God has given us. I declare that we have every spiritual resource as well, filled with righteousness, peace, and joy in the Holy Spirit.

I declare that we have an open Heaven, by the blood of Jesus, to get strategy and wisdom for how to advance each area that God has called us to. The Holy Spirit rests upon us and remains. We are keenly sensitive to the Lord and His voice. We ALL hear God's voice behind us, saying "This is the way; walk in it," and we never turn to the right or to the left. We hear God's voice clearly, and we follow Him. All of our prayers are heard and answered, and everything we need is provided in abundance.

I proclaim that You have given us ingenuity, inventiveness, and creativity and that we don't have to copy anyone else. You are giving us our own ministry culture, our own family structure, and our own unique talents, skills, and gifts. The atmosphere of Heaven saturates us and the people who are part of us. We are overshadowed by the Holy Spirit.

I declare that You are giving us favor with coaches, spiritual mothers and fathers, consultants, and contractors that will help us advance the mission You have given us.

I declare that no matter what kind of ministry we have, You are setting us up to be a spiritual house of prayer for all nations. We are in unity with Your worldwide voice that wants You to return, Jesus, and we will spare no energy as You spared no expense on the cross to bring Your inheritance.

I declare that we will be providers with the provision You bring. We will be givers, teachers, imparters, and be a great resource center to the world around us. We declare that our God provides all our needs according to His RICHES in glory in Christ Jesus.

AMEN!

*When it's hard and you are doubtful, give more.*

—Francis Chan

*When a poor person dies of hunger, it has not happened because God did not take care of him or her. It has happened because neither you nor I wanted to give that person what he or she needed.*

—Heidi Baker

*We are not to simply bandage the wounds of victims beneath the wheels of injustice, we are to drive a spoke into the wheel itself.*

—Dietrich Bonhoeffer

*God's personal, passionate concern for justice and righteousness was the starting place for His people to build them into every part of their culture. The place we should all live from is "justice and righteousness." Everything we do, from the way we raise our families to the way we run our businesses to our own relationships with the vulnerable, should reflect "justice and righteousness."*

—Jessica Nicholas

# PROVISION FOR THE POOR & ISSUES OF JUSTICE

*Share your food with the hungry!*
*Provide for the homeless*
*and bring them into your home!*
*Clothe the naked!*
*Don't turn your back on your own flesh and blood!*
*Then my favor will bathe you in sunlight*
*until you are like the dawn bursting through a dark night.*
*And then suddenly your healing will manifest.*
*You will see your righteousness march out before you,*
*and the glory of Yahweh will protect you from all harm!*
*Then Yahweh will answer you when you pray.*
*When you cry out for help, he will say,*
*'I am here.'*

Isaiah 58:7–9 (TPT)

*The generous will themselves be blessed, for*
*they share their food with the poor.*

Proverbs 22:9 (NIV)

*Those who give to the poor will lack nothing,*
*but those who close their eyes to them*
*receive many curses.*

Proverbs 28:27 (NIV)

# PROPHECY

I am the Provider for the poor, the orphan, the widow, the prisoner, the alien. I am the Provider for the economy, agriculture, animals, the environment, and everything I have created. On this side of eternity, I have economic justice that I am going to put on display for entire countries. I am not like man who brings well-intended, but impossible to execute, ideas. My love is practical and gives grace, decluttering complicated problems over justice issues with simple truths that work.

I am drafting every listening Christian to share part of the burden of My heart over a justice issue. The corporate church is about to become a provider, like Me, to the poor. Because of that, I will be able to share my glory with a generation. You will know who is walking with Me as people are awakened to love other people, because of My compassion. I am awakening this generation to be a solution generator, to show how My government is beautiful and works for the least and not just the greatest.

I am resetting the priorities of many so that they can see what I see, with new eyes. When I look at My beautiful earth, My heart is broken over the environment. My heart cries over the poor and the trafficked. I never look away from injustice and I am giving eyes to see what I see. I am sharing My burden with many. I will bring great provision so that something can be done. I have billions to solve water issues. I have billions to create sustainable food. I have the greatest strategies to create freedom for slaves. I have a justice system that is fair for prisoners caught in corruption. I have environmental plans to restore My earth in agriculture, oceans, and climate.

One of My provisions I am giving in this generation is celebrities, tech giants, royal family members, and politicians who will lend their influence as a resource to My people. I want to show a generation what justice looks like within national problems and social issues. I have spoken My dreams of civil rights through prophets before, but I am providing the vision and strategy to manifest those dreams. I have given awareness about issues of extreme hunger, but I am raising up scientists and manufacturers to develop food sources that are sustainable for the poor and distribution methods that can curb corruption. I am launching curriculum for education, married to technology, that can go into any country and raise up a generation of leaders in war-torn and developing nations where education has failed over and over.

Today, you may feel like the issues are too big, but I invite you to look into My eyes of love. I have created a universe that I don't even fully fit into because I cannot be contained by space. But I live in your love, in your heart. I am commissioning My love and it will look like justice to the oppressed.

# PRAYER

God, my Provider, share the burden of Your heart with me. Help me to take off a bite-sized piece of Your heart and then bring me into alignment with the tribe of people who are already tackling that issue with Your resources and love.

Draft me into Your justice army, show me who You are calling me to love. Help me to carry people with Your compassion.

I invite You to use popular culture, books, movies, stories, and even firsthand accounts to pursue me and define in me a well of compassion. Give me as much as I can handle.

God, I love Your people and everything You have created. Give me strategies and finances to help in real ways. I want to leave a legacy of saved lives, educated children, freed slaves, economic and social justice, well-stewarded agriculture, loved widows, and healed land. God, thank you that in Job 27, he defines why You gave him favor, and it was because he had your Fathers's heart for the poor and for his land and animals. Help me meet those qualifications for Your favor. Help me to walk in Your love of justice.

My Provider, help me not fall in the trap of humanism and hyper-socialistic thinking or conspiracy over what You have created.

Let me walk in balanced love, slow to anger, long-suffering patience, but real action. Create in me the heart of a provider as You are a Provider, so that in my lifetime I will touch justice issues in real ways. Multiply the little in my life so that it has huge implications on lives that would never be touched if I didn't say yes. Let me live the life that pleases You and reap the benefits of it that are laid out in Isaiah 58.

AMEN!

# DECLARATION

Created from Isaiah 58 in the Passion Translation

I declare I will live the kind of fasted life that God desires. I will remove heavy chains of oppression. I will help fight for economic justice. I will set free the crushed and mistreated. I will be used to break off the yoke of injustice.

> *"This is the kind of fast that I desire:*
> *Remove the heavy chains of oppression!*
> *Stop exploiting your workers!*
> *Set free the crushed and mistreated!*
> *Break off every yoke of bondage!*

I commit to share my food with the hungry. I will powerfully impact the homeless and share space with them in my heart and help them find security. I will bring clothes and provision to those who don't have any. I will not turn away from family members in poverty or who are marginalized because of addictions, lifestyle, or poverty.

*Share your food with the hungry!*
*Provide for the homeless*
*and bring them into your home!*
*Clothe the naked!*
*Don't turn your back on your own flesh and blood!*

I declare that God's favor will bathe me in sunlight, that I will be like the dawn bursting through the dark night. I will have healing in my household and things that were unjust in my own life will turn around. I declare that God will protect me from harm.

*Then my favor will bathe you in sunlight*
*until you are like the dawn bursting*
*through a dark night.*
*And then suddenly your healing will manifest.*
*You will see your righteousness march out before you,*
*and the glory of Yahweh will protect you from all harm!*

I declare that, as I love the poor, it creates more openness to hear God and be close to His heart. I will prophetically understand His will for my life more clearly. I commit to not speak negatively against others, even in general ways against oppressed people, and even when what they do is evil.

*Then Yahweh will answer you when you pray*
*When you cry out for help, he will say,*
*'I am here.'*
*If you banish every form of oppression,*
*the scornful accusations,*
*and vicious slander.*

I declare that I will offer myself to acts of compassion, to not look away when I see people in misery, but to seek God's heart even if all I can do is pray in the moment. I proclaim His light will rise in the dark areas of my life and He will give me clarity of purpose.

*and if you offer yourselves in compassion for the hungry*
*and relieve those in misery,*
*then your dawning light will rise in the darkness*
*and your gloom will turn into noonday splendor!*

I declare that my Provider will give me plans and guidance as part of His provision as I love those who are oppressed. He will give me full strength and cause His fruit to multiply in my life.

*Yahweh will always guide you*
*where to go and what to do.*
*He will fill you with refreshment*

> *even when you are in a dry, difficult place.*
> *He will continually restore strength to you,*
> *so you will flourish like a well-watered garden*
> *and like an ever-flowing, trustworthy spring of blessing.*

I proclaim that God is using me to rebuild broken systems, repair cities, and restore communities!

> *Your people will rebuild long-deserted ruins,*
> *building anew on foundations laid long before you.*
> *You will be known as Repairers of the Cities*
> *and Restorers of Communities.*

I declare that I will pursue God's desires, especially when I have a different agenda. I will lay it down for His agenda. I will not make commitments toward the poor or with my resources that I cannot keep. I will commit to simple acts of love and obedience.

> *If you stop pursuing your own desires on my holy day,*
> *and refrain from disregarding the Sabbath,*
> *if you call the Sabbath a delightful pleasure*
> *and Yahweh's holy day honorable,*
> *if you honor it properly by*
> *not chasing your own desires,*
> *serving your own interests, and speaking empty words...*

I declare that because I am walking with God, loving the poor, and caring about justice that I will find Heavenly joy that only comes from living this way! I will prosper and be highly favored!

>...*then you will find the joyous bliss*
>*that comes from serving Yahweh.*
>*And I will cause you to prosper*
>*and be carried triumphantly over*
>*the high places of the land.*
>*You will enjoy the heritage of Jacob, your ancestor."*
>*Certainly the mouth of Yahweh has spoken it!*

*It is the duty of all Nations to acknowledge the providence of Almighty God, to obey His will, to be grateful for His benefits, and humbly to implore His protection and favor.*

—George Washington

*One of the exciting benefits of this revelation is that financial harvests are not seasonal. If you give, you will receive! You may not receive the harvest immediately, but if you plant, you will always be on the receiving end. The Word says to cast your bread on the water and after many days it will return to you (Ecclesiastes 11:1).*

—Kenneth Copeland

*The Lord is your Provider. He loves you and He has a good plan for your life. He wants to bless you so you can fulfill His plan and purpose … so you can really enjoy your life. And in His Word, He tells us who He is and how we can access everything we need through Christ.*

—Joyce Meyer

*Never be afraid to trust an unknown future to a known God.*

—Corrie ten Boom

# PROVISION FOR DESTINY

*A thief has only one thing in mind—he wants to steal, slaughter, and destroy. But I have come to give you everything in abundance, more than you expect—life in its fullness until you overflow!*

John 10:10 (TPT)

*Trust in the Lord completely,
and do not rely on your own opinions.
With all your heart rely on him to guide you,
and he will lead you in every decision you make.
Become intimate with him in whatever you do,
and he will lead you wherever you go.*

Proverbs 3:5–6 (TPT)

*Make God the utmost delight and
pleasure of your life,
and he will provide for you what you desire the most.
Give God the right to direct your life,
and as you trust him along the way
you'll find he pulled it off perfectly!*

Psalm 37:4–5 (TPT)

# PROPHECY

As a Provider, I created you with this huge space within you. I call it My temple. I will fill it with My Spirit over and over, and you will be a well of provision. Everything you need to fulfill your destiny is provided for. Fall in love with those you are called to and you will manifest finances and glory that the world isn't worthy of.

I want you to see yourself holding the keys to My Kingdom. I want you to feel as though the most important, wealthy person, who has the biggest platform of your generation, just put these keys in your hand and they are real keys to real resources. I am calling you to see through My eyes of love to see what doors your life will unlock. Your life is a key to so many coming into the Kingdom.

Even if you are thriving in your destiny there is more. I don't just want to add to you, I want to multiply you. If you have faith for something, I want you to spend time with Me and let Me expand your faith even more. I will do beyond what you can hope for or dream of, but I want to do it through intentional partnership. I want to show you how to partner step-by-step with Me. I don't just want to bring revelation so you will do something for Me, I want you to know Me so intimately so we can do it together. I want to bring so much unity to you, and the people I am calling you to love, that you will feel like you aren't running on batteries but you are plugged into an unlimited power source.

I want to give you the resource of a full life; it was always My desire. Some good Christian people will think you are exaggerating My passion for you, or that you are delusional in your faith, but I will use your radical faith to make history.

I want to give you the role of provider for others. Just as Jehovah-Jireh is one of My names, one of the ways to access Me, I want to make you a resource center for those around you. You will help many people become My vision on the earth. Don't look to others as if you needed a provider, I have made you a benefactor of My provision. Don't be a victim of lack, I will give you strategy for all that I have for you.

When I created you, I created a perfect plan of provision. Just like when you had your children and began savings accounts for school, stocked up on groceries, planned trips and vacations, classes and skills training, I prepared everything you would need to walk in the fullness of My Son, Jesus.

Access My plan, know Me as your full Provider. Ask, seek, and knock and I will give you everything you ask for, in light of My precious Son.

# PRAYER

God, help me to see, through Your eyes, the ones I am called to love. Give me a vision of my family, the people group I am most called to, the city, geography, country, industry, ministry You have prepared for me. Show me the ones You love and let me fall in love with them. I will lean into Your heart as a Provider and become a conduit of this provision for them. Thank you for all those who have already gone before me in this destiny. Help me to build on their legacy and inherit from what they have already harvested.

Thank you that there have already been two thousand years of Christianity and that one generation is going to inherit in areas that have been prayed over for all those years. Help me to inherit from those prayers and take Your Gospel of love further throughout my life. Pour out the provision of legacy on my life. I cry out like Elisha, give me a double portion, God, so that I can do more than I ever hoped or imagined. Help me to be focused on Your dreams, not mine.

God, I know that my destiny is full of provision, help me to not be afraid or doubtful. Heal any unbelief in me so that I can access the riches of Your glory and bring transformation to the world. When I feel limited to my rolodex, and what my skills and talents and gifts can produce, help me to lean into You and allow Your strength to cover my weakness. Help me to not focus on myself, but to focus on You and Your glorious nature within me. Give me faith for all You have called me to.

Jesus, I receive the provision that You restored me to at the cross and resurrection. I don't want even one drop of Your blood to be wasted, but I want to live in the fullness of what You intended before You even created me. I align my faith with Your promise for every provision for my life and my destiny in You.

AMEN!

# DECLARATION

I declare that for every part of my destiny there is a provision. There are actual resources for everything I am called to and I release them now in the name of Jesus!

I release finances, properties, skill, talent, social capital, contractors, coaches, contracts, permits, anything that is needed for what I am called to, let it come forth in its time!

I declare that I am fearfully and wonderfully made by a Provider who is my Father, and that He has a perfect plan of provision so that everything He put inside of me can find its full expression and release in this lifetime and in eternity with Him.

I proclaim that I am also a provider, and that my life will release great resources to the world around me.

HALLELUJAH!